Home to Saskatchewan

Muriel J. Montbriand

All the photos are of my husband's and my uncles who served in World War II (1939-1945).

ISBN-13: 978-1500374266

ISBN-10: 1500374261

Copyright © 2014 Muriel J. Montbriand
All Rights Reserved

The findings provided in this book have been
made possible through two research grants
awarded to:
Muriel J. Montbriand Ph.D., Reg.N.
by Health Services Utilization and Research
Commission, Saskatchewan, Canada, years 1998
to 2000 and 2001 to 2003

Dedication

To my husband Fred, and my two sons,
John and James

Special thanks to Mrs. Gibson.

Special thanks also goes to
James I. Montbriand MA for designing the cover
for this book. All the photos are of my husband's
and my uncles who served in
World War Two.

Forward

The 'voices' you will read in this book are real, actual quotes. These stories contain the actual words of participants from a two-phase research study conducted by myself with the help of a research assistant.

All names attached to these stories 'voices' are pseudonyms. I have eliminated most small town names given by the storytellers but have included the names of the two largest cities in Saskatchewan plus names of some of the military training bases mentioned. In a number of stories I have intertwined stories of two voices that told similar stories. Other stories, I have taken literary license by including additional characters who are listeners (the listeners in the interviews were of course my research assistant or myself). However, these added listener characters are usually not actual persons attached to the participants' stories, but I emphasize again, the 'voices' are actual quotes.

All data for these research projects were collected beginning in 1998. After analysis of the first part of this study, I received the second grant, a stand-alone research, in 2001, to specifically analyze the life history stories provided by these seniors in the original research, 1998 to 2000:

Seniors' Perceptions and Meanings of Illness and Healing
    Socio-Health Research Grant
    (over two years) 1998 – 2000)
    Source: Health Services Utilization and Research
    Commission, Saskatchewan, Canada

Life History and Illness Connections: Seniors' Perspectives
    Socio-Health Research Grant
    (over two years 2001 – 2003)
    Source: Health Services Utilization and Research
    Commission, Saskatchewan, Canada

Two research articles were published in refereed journals from the above second analysis of the life histories exclusively. For your interest, these are as follows:

Montbriand, M. J. (2004) Seniors' Survival Trajectories and the Illness Connection. ***Qualitative Health Research, 14,*** 449-461

Montbriand, M. J. (2004) Seniors' Life Histories and Perceptions of Illness. **Western Journal of Nursing Research, 26,** 242-260

The purpose of this research was to examine senior's perceptions of how or if illness and life history were related. The topics covered during the interviews included seniors' perceived cause of their illness, best sources of information about their illness and why they liked those sources, what kinds of therapies they prescribed for themselves. We asked each senior to tell their life history plus how they connected their life history to their illness. The randomly selected sample of 190 seniors all lived independently in a Canadian prairie city and were 60 years of age or older. The actual interviews were an average of two hours and seventeen minutes (Range: maximum time, 3 hr., 3 min., minimum time, 32 min.). The thirty-two minute interview was with a senior that my assistant sent to the hospital emergency department. Both my assistant and I were registered nurses at the time of the research, now retired.

Over the years I have often felt haunted by these 'voices.' In truth, something in my heart kept urging me and indeed began shouting that these 'voices' needed to be heard. The sheer enormity of providing a publication using the total one hundred and ninety random sampled participants' 'voices' overwhelmed me.

However, recently I realized:

* first, that the stories in this research were so diverse that they could not be contained in one theme for a book. Therefore, one theme had to be selected.

* Second, and probably most important, I recalled that a number of these seniors provided diverse and interesting personal experiences of the war years.

I don't intend to analyze this set of voices presented here. You as the readers may have that luxury, if you wish. And yet, I cannot refrain from adding just a few clarifications here and there in brackets. As well, I would like to provide you with just a few thoughts that struck me as I read these voices again after a space of sixteen years.

First, I noticed what a long and ardurous journey it had been for all of these people, what a long, long journey home to Saskatchewan. I also noticed how often the pain and suffering of many service men was described. This mental suffering we probably now would label as PTSD, post-traumatic stress disorder, but in the post-war years it was called shell shock.

Most of all, I noticed again how the war experience for these men had altered others lives. This altering especially affected the wives and sweethearts of these returned soldiers. Perhaps not so surprising, women who became war brides or simply who lived in the midst of the war in England and Europe also came to Saskatchewan to find a home. All of these also had stories to tell.

During the interviews, I often wondered at how few of the men wanted to specifically talk about what happened to them in the war. Often they skirted around that subject by just saying a few words. Of course, in contrast to this one or two of the men presented stories that were quite cavalier.

But, I did say, I wouldn't analyze. Most of these wonderful people are now dead. Yet, I still puzzle over their 'voices.' Their stories need to be remembered. As in all wars, and all wars are horrific, it's a long way home.

M.J.M

VOICES

Adam
Norah
Kate
Fay
Mel
Ned
Amelia
Frank
Henry
Pauline
Anna
Elizabeth
Patrick
Bernadette
Louise
Russell
Lara
Hildegarde

Adam

The first thing he said was, "I was in England during the war." Not that it was such a startling statement, but it was the way he said it and smiled. In fact, he was the sort of man who smiled a lot and made you wonder what his life had been like.

Then he began again, "When I was forty years old my brother and I, we had a garage and implement business out at small town Saskatchewan.

"The army got me in 1943. I was gone almost three years. When I came back my brother and I managed to get a service station. We ran that for ten years. My brother's health started to fail a little bit so we got out of there. We didn't know what to do, but all my life I had a yen to go into accounting. I managed to get in with a firm of Chartered Accountants. I took a five-year correspondence course. I wrote the CA exams and I passed the first time. I was forty-six when I became a Chartered Accountant. Now, uh, I felt good about that. I've felt good about it ever since. Every time I stop and think about it I think well at age forty that took something a little above the ordinary."

He stopped and leaned back in his chair. The light breeze was ruffling his now greying hair and one had to think that he was still a pretty handsome fellow. His whole self exuded a sort of contentment, and he continued, "That's the way I felt about my whole life. Uh, I can honestly say I don't think I ever failed at anything. Uh, we made a success of that business. It was our Dad's business. He died when I was sixteen and my brother was twenty. Actually then it was mother's business, but she couldn't have run it without us. We took over and paid her out. We made a success of it.

"I got into the army. I even had a session of that. They made a surveyor out of me. I never got to use it because I, when I was fully trained the war was over. But at least I made a success of it. We came back. We ran the service station downtown. And then I became a Chartered

Accountant through sweat and toil, and I felt I made a success of that, so . . . " He drifted off into his thoughts, but then he shook his head and went on, "But when I became a Chartered Accountant it was like a new lease on life.

"I guess I told you, in 1943 I got drafted into the army. And my brother was old enough that he could have avoided it, but when I was going, it would have left him with a monumental task of keeping the business going. So he decided to hell with it, 'I'll go too.' Yah, that's what he said," and he kinda chuckled to himself.

"He joined the Air Force and when we were discharged we started over again. We had sold the garage. I was married by then, and my wife and I had two little boys.

"I think I'm getting ahead of myself in telling you my story, so let me back up a bit. When I went away to war, I couldn't just leave my wife out at that little town. There was no doctor out there, and in the wintertime the roads were closed. I moved her into Saskatoon. When I came home in 1946, I joined her here in Saskatoon, and I never left. My brother and I got a service station downtown, and we ran it for ten years. We did very well. In ten years my wife and I had enough to buy this house and I made enough to finance my six years of education to become a Chartered Accountant, and I told you I got my CA."

Then he suddenly leaned forward, picked up his coffee cup, took a sip, and his blue eyes sparkled like stars, "But I didn't tell you the best part yet. I mean how I met my wife. She was from the next town to where my family lived, where we had our garage, and she was a schoolteacher. She taught school halfway between my hometown and this bigger town, ten miles from both. And in the fall of 1936 the school had a Halloween dance, and I went out to that dance with a bunch of other young bucks from town. I think I had met her before that but that's the first time I can really remember her. They raffled off a box of apples. Tickets were ten cents and I won the apples. And I've joked many times that I didn't know then that the school ma'am came with the apples.

"But anyway, I never, I don't think I ever saw her again. That was in October of 1936. I don't think I saw her again until the Sports Day in (town) on the 24th of May. That was in 1937. I hitchhiked over to what we called the big town, back then. At the dance that night, I asked her for lunch, and by God if she didn't accept. I didn't realize until afterwards that she was sucking for a ride back out to the school. She had to teach the next day. I bummed a ride back home too and got a ride for her back out to her school.

"Anyway, once she stumbled across my path the second time, I was sucked in. I'll tell you, what a doll she was. I'll show you these pictures," and he was up out of his chair in a shot, grabbed an album from the bookshelf, "That's us taken in 1937."

He was smiling at the picture, "Yeah, we got married in June 1939, and the war broke out in September of 39. Well I probably should have joined up then, but with a brand new bride especially like her, who's going to go away and leave her. Well then the first thing there was a child came and then, another one. But before the second one came, I was already drafted. And I had to go then. I went down to Petawawa to get my basic training and when my basic training was over then's when the army decided to make a surveyor out of me, and that of course was six months. Well I was so damn lonesome by that time. That's when I found out I was going to be in Canada for another six months. I told her and the boys to come there. They had good bus service, and with a little skullduggery and help from some of my friends, I think I only spent three or four nights away from her in the six months she was down there. But guess what, she got pregnant just before I was shipped overseas." He took a deep sigh. "So our daughter was a year old before I saw her."

Again he was leaning back in his chair, a far away look in his eyes. "What a life we've had. It had a few dark spots in it, but most of it's been bright. I didn't get my discharge until 46.

"I tell you, back there when we were courting, while I was waiting for her to say yes. I tell you I had to be quite a salesman to get her to agree. She didn't just fall into my arms. No way. I had to be a real salesman to get her to come along and get onboard ship.

"That was the most important thing in my whole life, I didn't realize how important it was until after I had found her. I mean I wasn't looking for a life partner. She, as I said a couple of times, she just blundered into my path and once she was there, I wasn't about to let her go. Life is good."

Norah

"It was kind of a love story you could say. I met him on Christmas Eve. He was just everything that a woman would want. He was kind, and compassionate, loving, caring, just a wonderful guy. I'd seen him before but I didn't know who he was. I was stationed, that is there was an air base here, the Air Force was stationed here at that time. Well my boyfriend at that time was a Mounty and he wouldn't leave me alone, so I went away. I literally looked out of town for a job. I was fed up. I decided I didn't want anything to do with any man. I said to my sister, 'I'm going to be an old maid, I'm not getting married.'

"But then I met Ken and I got married to him. My sister said, 'You don't even know him,' but I said, 'I know I like him,' and that was it. We were so happy."

Why did this bring a tear to her eye?

"You see he was already in the Air Force when I met him, and then he went overseas. At first I wasn't really scared, but you know we probably didn't hear everything that was going on over there. Then finally the war was over. He came back, but it wasn't really over because he decided to stay in the Air Force.

"You know, to begin with, I really wasn't sure about it all, but he stayed on, and we were going over to Europe. And I began to just love it.

"Ken was on exchange with NATO and NORAD. We were all over Europe, and I met so many, many wonderful friends. We were having such a wonderful time. Ken and I had two little girls over there, and Ken, well he had a wonderful sense of humor. He wasn't a practical joker type. Don't get me wrong. He was one of those, he was like a ray of sunshine on a gloomy day.

"And there were so many wonderful parties, always parties. And many other wives and I, well it was just like "Sound of Music," or

"American In Paris." I enjoyed it so much. That was our life and it really was a wonderful life."

Now the tear had turned to two and more.

"I'm sorry," she struggled to get a Kleenex. Finally, with tears streaming down her face, she continued, "We retired and came back home, to here."

Then she started again, "It's a year ago now, but it seems like yesterday. Everything seemed fine. I was going out to my regular bridge club, and we only had one car. So he said he wanted to go down to the store, so he drove me and told me he would pick me up around five..."

She was looking into space.

"When he wasn't there, it was so unusual, because he always was so prompt. Always on time. It was a passion with him to be on time. And he didn't come. I phoned. No answer. I didn't know what to do. Finally my friend drove me home."

Here she stopped. After a while she got up and walked to the window.

"He committed suicide. Shot himself…"

It was some time before she finally said, "He was in the pilot training program with NATO and NORAD. Maybe it was when he had to go after a crash. All the mutilated bodies. All the body parts. I don't know. Maybe it was something from the war. I don't know. He saw a lot of horror. He never talked . . . about it. I never even knew he was depressed."

Kate

"We never wasted a thing. I still make my own five quarts of soup. It will do me about three weeks. Tomorrow is soup day. I make it so there is no fat in it or nothing. It's just vegetables, I buy a bunch of celery and cut it up and freeze it, and I got that: celery, cabbage and onions and a few carrots, and you know, it's beautiful soup. There's no extra salt in it because I use Mrs. Dash all the time.

"I was born in England, and I came over here and worked as a hired girl. I came with my family of course, mom and dad. My mom died, so here's my dad with four kids, twelve, one, seven and four. Not a relative in the country. They were all in England. Unbelievable. So I quit school then and looked after the house, raised my brothers and went back to school for more years and got my grade eight.

"Then my stepmother handed me some aprons and she said, 'You'll need these,' and sent me out to work. Monday morning that was. Yes, dad got a new wife. I'm sure it was a marriage of convenience, cause she had two children. Her husband was killed, and dad had four more with her. It never lasted very long, and I'm sure that's why. But yes, we all went out to work when we were fourteen years old. But we learned not to waste a thing. That's just my way of life.

"I went out to work at one place in the district. They were farmers, and they had two sons. I married one of them, and that was during the war years in 39. And then I traveled around with him, and he was stationed at different places. Then he went overseas in 44. My girl was only three weeks old, and he was over there for 18 months until 45. Then we came to Saskatchewan.

"We started on the farm. We had nothing really. The first two years we didn't have a car or nothing, you know. Twenty miles from a doctor, no phone, but there's thousand's of stories like that. It sure teaches you for life. I'm telling you. You're so grateful for everything. In my day a handshake was as good as a signed agreement, you know.

"I remember when things were pretty rough with Tom's drinking, and I went to the library and got this book "Grow Up and Live." When I read that book, it made me put up with it, the drinking that is, and go on with my life.

"When I look back, I had tunnel vision, cause I had three kids to support and pay the bills, but I had no choice. I was tired all the time from working heavy work, and I couldn't think, there was no time to think ahead. There was no money. You just looked straight ahead. You made sure you paid all the bills

"You know back in those days, if you didn't have a partner or married by age of twenty-one, there was something wrong with you. That was the lifestyle then. To begin with the first thing was finding an occupation, then raising a family, success in work, and then health concerns and then loss, death.

"My husband died, and I looked after my mother-in-law until she died. She died in the house. I looked after my husband. He died in the house. I looked after my father. He died in our house. I guess the most important thing was keeping a roof over our heads, food on the table, you know, it's all you work for."

Fay

"I was in the Air Force during the war, in Britain. I had met my husband before the war. We were married in 1942. He was an engineer on the railroad and they wouldn't let him go to the war. Everyone except him was in the forces, and he felt bad.

"Then I found out I was pregnant in 1944 and they discharged me from duty. I was in Edinburgh then. I was stationed all over, and, yes, my husband was in Edinburgh. We came to Canada in 1952, and that was a big decision.

"When my husband died, the bottom fell out of my world. But then you have to pick up the pieces."

Mel

"I finished high school and war was on and everybody was going to get a call eventually, and I said, 'To hell with it. I'll beat them to it.' So I joined up.

"I joined up in artillery and trained in artillery and went overseas and then trained another month over there. That's when we were qualified as gunners. They said we need infantry, you, you, and you. And I was a you, and I landed up in the Regina Rifles Regiment.

"I was in the front line.

"I got hit, a month before the war was over. And then I got stuck in England for a year after the war.

"I was wounded in the leg.

"After I got hit, I walked back to the line.

"And from the line we went to the first aid, and eventually we landed back in the hospital and had surgery there.

"I came back to Canada and stayed in the military. Took an officer's course and met my wife at the air force base in Moose Jaw.

"Being in the military, there are rules and as long as everybody plays by them, and I liked the service. I just liked it, and there was no reason to get out when you enjoy what you're doing."

Ned

June first, and it was a sunny day. Tom was putting in bedding plants, but when he saw Ned just sitting on his deck. Well he looked sort of sad, so Tom went over and joined him. As he sat on one of the wicker chairs, he noticed the trowel and tray of bedding plants sitting at the edge of his neighbor's deck, ready to go.

"So I see you're about to start planting too," Tom nodded. "Martha's gone off to pick up some more geraniums, and I think she's expecting that I'll have all those petunias in by the time she gets back."

Ned just sat there looking off into the distance.

"Hey, Ned," Tom stared at his neighbor of thirty years, "Anything wrong?"

Quickly Ned, turned, "Nah, just thinking. Today's our anniversary."

"So congratulations."

"Fifty-two years now," Ned said pensively, "and here I sit, three kids and one nagging wife later."

"Awe, come on Ned."

It was then that Ned turned to face his long time friend and neighbor. His expression was somber, and Tom was a bit surprised, cause he seldom saw Ned like this.

"You know," Ned continued, "I picked Sal out from across the room. It was at a dance. She was cute. I was in the aircrew at that time. I was a young man then.

"At that age when you are getting married, you don't look that far down the line. War was bad, real bad." He glanced at his friend, "I guess you know that. You were there too. It was very bad. The war was bad," he repeated, "but it was also very romantic. I'd come and see her, you know, and then we parted at the train, and then I was gone for a long time again, and that was overseas. You know, it was sort of romantic love that you saw in the movies. And we got together, and then I was away again, and then we got together." He took a deep breath and blew it out slowly. "And then I said, 'Lets just get married. You know I can't stand this any longer,' and that's about the way it went."

Suddenly Sal was there with a couple of cups of coffee for them. She plunked them on the patio table in front of Tom and Ned. Tom eyed her thoughtfully as he watched her stand there with her hands on her hips. He guessed that she had been standing at the patio door listening to what Ned just said. She confirmed that guess by what she said next: "In our generation, we were fully committed," Sal began with that feisty smile of hers. "We were raised in an environment where you stayed with your marriage. It was a disgrace to leave. Where as today, well, no disgrace in a divorce."

Sal left, and Ned continued as though she hadn't even been there, "You know, Tom, I often think of the chain of events. If I hadn't got scarlet fever and delayed staying overseas. I wouldn't have been around."

"You mean to get married?" Tom almost whispered.

But Ned didn't seem to care if Sal heard what he was saying. He just continued on musing in his usual voice, "People believe in fate, and I wonder some times, and also how fate was at work. Well, I'm saying where there'd be times when there would be two things in a row and things just happen, but they don't necessarily need to happen that way."

"I'm going to walk out on you, one of these days," Sal called through the kitchen window. Obviously she had been listening in on the conversation, but now she turned on the taps and was banging around with the pots and pans.

"We got married on June first." Ned continued, "Married now for fifty-two years. Back then after the war, I wanted to go to university. I had an ultimate dream then. I'd do it my way, an absolute dream."

Sal was hanging out the window again, "He's the guy that had three kids and a stay at home mom to look after them. Financially there is no way that his dream was, or is, going to come true. But he stuck to his guns and supported his family. Even if there were lousy jobs that he had to have. He had stressful jobs, pillar to post just to make a living, taking pay cuts, jobs closing down, and here we are sitting, but we are probably better off than a lot of poor people. We have pensions, and that's not great, but they give us a comfortable living."

Tom looked from Sal to Ned, and really wanted to move off the deck and get on with his planting but . . .

Finally Sal moved away from the window and Ned continued, "At first, it was a love story holding us together, now we're stuck together by crazy glue."

Amelia

"My dad lived to be 104, and do you know he went through World War One, and he came home safe and sound. He got married again. But she didn't like me."

'Who didn't like you?' I wondered who she meant, but she must have sensed my wondering.

"The woman he married." She said this with a smirk and then continued, "My dad liked me so much. He used to put his arms around me, and that made her so mad."

She must have meant her stepmother. When two people are talking, it seems amazing how the speaker will often let the listener fill in words for them. Without even noticing my puzzlement, Amelia carried on:

"She just hated me, and I was scared of her. I thought she would kill me, or something. She hated me so much. She was just jealous, I guess. Of course, she wasn't very good looking and everybody said I was so nice looking."

I had to smile, because she had been able to meet the sixty-five-age requirement for the study, and Amelia was still a fine looking woman. She was sitting very primly in her chair. Obviously she had just gotten her hair done. It was a silvery white color. Her whole demeanor spoke of a woman who took pride in looking well.

"When my dad was in the war, and I was too young to remember that. I stayed with my oldest sister. After the war my dad married over there."

'England?' I ventured.

"Yes. Yes, he surprised us. And surprised my stepmother, I guess, and she was supposed to know that he had children. She didn't know that he had any children when she married him, and she just hated me.

"Then I married Foster. He was from the states, and when he joined the Air Force he had to take out his Canadian citizenship.

"The night I was having our first baby, he ran out into our street, and he was running up and down the street yelling, 'Amelia's having a baby and I don't know what to do!' Course when we were on the farm, it was always the women who came when a woman was having a baby. The men never came into the house then. They all went down to the barn. But here in the city, he just didn't know what he was suppose to do."

I was laughing with Amelia. She had such a lovely laugh.

"I had the most wonderful, wonderful, husband. Oh he was so lovely and that's why I don't want to leave this house. I have such fond memories of him here. When he came back from World War Two, then I got pregnant again.

"He joined up with the military again and went to Korea. When he came home he died, full of cancer. He worked as a mechanic when he came back at last."

Amazing to sum up their life in such a few short sentences. And yet, hadn't she said it all. I was almost surprised when she continued:

"He use to always sing to me, and I would sing along while he was driving.

"One day after he had his stroke, and he was in this chair in the front room, and I said something, and he kind of got mad at me. Then I came into the kitchen and when I came out and turned the corner and he started to sing, 'Let me call you sweetheart, I'm in love with you,' and he hugged me. Oh I thought he was going to kill me, he squeezed me so hard.

"We never stopped liking each other.

"He died when he was eighty-three years, and he was three years older than me."

Frank

"A day in the army. I can just visualize that exactly. You know what those guys, NCO's are like? Stand right in front of your face and just holler at you and you don't dare say a word.

"After overseas, I just wanted to do anything, just get me out of the services. And I swore to God that I'd never work for anybody after that. I was going to work for myself.

"But I did work for different people in my home town, grocery store, hardware store, service station. Finally this guy asked me if I'd work for him. And I said sure I'd work for him in his garage. About a year later, well I met Beatrice.

"But then this garage-guy let me go from work because I'd taken off to Saskatoon to get a ring for her, Beatrice that is. He told me, 'At the end of the month, you're through.' I said, 'Fine, if that's the kind of guy you are, that's good.'

"So then I went back and helped dad on the farm and then I come back with a magneto off the tractor. It was the same garage but it was all rebuilt. I knew the old mechanic there, and I said, 'Can you fix this magneto?' He says, 'Sure but you better come to work for this guy.' He says, 'Go and ask him.' So I did, and he was in there alone and he said, 'No, I don't need any help right now.' So that night at about ten o'clock at night, he phoned me and said, 'Would you like to come to work tomorrow morning?' He must have talked to the mechanic.

"So I worked for him for a year and then he asked me to go into business with him as his partner. Well what the heck? I can't afford to go into business with him. I'd sure like to. So I got some help from Beatrice's dad and went into business. Then we expanded to the next town. We had another outlet in the next town, which was twenty-five miles away.

"So I continued back and forth, back and forth. My job was to go out on the road and sell, and he looked after the internal things. Then we had a propane explosion in the garage and that kind of upset things. Then my partner wanted to go elsewhere, and he said, 'You buy me out because you know the business.'

"So I bought him out, and we did well for eight years. Then I sold the business and was a butcher for a year and a half, till our daughter was through grade twelve.

"Then we moved into the city. So I went to work in a big garage. Then they wanted me to sell cars, and I said, 'No.' So any ways . . . That's the way it went.

*

"Now back then, when I got out of the services, I was so nervous. Some times I'd have nightmares about, you know, over there, the war. I guess I was close to a nervous breakdown.

"Beatrice just had a new baby. The work at the garage, like I told you, I was working and it wasn't going good. I guess this was all new to me, and I guess maybe the strain was getting to me. I was scared to go home at night for fear that I might choke her and choke the baby.

"Yah, really. That bad.

"I was really scared. I doctored for a while, and he more or less got tired of me and he said, 'Well you know,' he says, 'I can't help you anymore.' He more or less said it was all in my head. I did get some medication, tranquilizers. But I eventually quit taking them.

"I was just scared, scared of what! I can't tell you."

Henry

Just when spring has finally arrived on the prairie, winter is back, and that's the way it was the frosty morning they left to pick up Henry after the war.

Margaret Ann and her brother, Ted, had to start out early because it was a three-hour drive from the farm to Regina. But she had to be up early anyway because she had to start the fire in the cook stove in the kitchen plus make the oatmeal for breakfast. She knew that her mom was getting frail since her last bout of pneumonia, so she wanted to fix some sandwiches for her to have with her tea later in the day. It seemed like forever getting her mom washed and dressed this morning, but she tried not to look like she was hurrying her.

"You run along and get ready, dear. I know you're so anxious to meet your young man again," her mom told her.

After she made sure there was enough wood for the day by the stove, she made up a lunch for herself and Ted, something they could eat when they were on the road. Then she had to get properly dress cause she wanted to look good for Henry. Quickly she slipped on her navy blue dress that she usually wore to church on Sunday then her warm wool coat that was a bit short for that dress, but would have to do. Better to be warm than cold. Most important, she slipped on her engagement ring. She didn't always wear it when she was cleaning at Walkers Drug Store. Didn't want to damage or lose that diamond. She smiled at it lovingly. The diamond was so small but so beautiful. She took a deep sigh, 'He's coming home. He's safely home at last.'

Every morning since he left for the war, she had made time to slip into the church and pray that he would be safe, that he would return to her. And now was that day at last. Mister Walker at the Drug Store had been so good to her, letting her take the day off. Course it was to be expected, it would be without pay, but just to go along with Ted and see Henry at last. It waall worth it. She actually had butterflies in her stomach.

"Hay, are you coming," it was Ted calling to her from the door, and she could hear the old car rumbling outside.

As she jumped into the car Ted turned to her, 'Now, you know you may have to sit in the back when we come back with Henry. He'll probably not fit in the back."

She nodded at him. "Of course. Do you know where we are picking him up?"

"Yah, he told me HighFin, a pub on South Railway. Didn't have much time on the phone cause you know how much long distance costs. I think I know how to find it. He says it has a big lighted up sign and there'll be lots of military guys around there anyway if we don't find it right away. 'Just ask,' he says."

Margaret Ann quickly swallowed her disappointment. She had hoped Henry would suggest they go to a café and have something to eat. But, she just shrugged her shoulders. It would be a long drive and best to get back before dark.

*

But when they got to Regina around one o'clock, there was no sign of Henry along South Railway or at the HighFin pub. Lots of soldiers were milling around and looked like they were having a lot of fun shouting and joking with each other.

Ted and Margaret Ann decided to go and fill up the car with gas and have a bite to eat at a cheap little café. Around about four o'clock they tried again. Ted parked the car and told Margaret Ann he'd just have a look. Margaret Ann sat in the car trying not to shiver. She even bent her head and said a prayer, trying to quell her anxiety. But then when she looked up, there he was coming out the door of the HighFin. He was wearing his sheepskin leather jacket from the Air Force. Oh he looked so handsome, so . . . Her heart skipped a beat, and she jumped out of the car as they reached her.

What a wonderful moment!

Henry grabbed her and kissed her. Suddenly Margret Ann was startled. His kiss was so rough. He smelled of beer.

"Gosh your skinny," Henry laughed.

"It's so wonderful to have you home," she gasped trying hard to smile and not let him see how startled she had felt.

"We better not waste time," Ted was already warning them. "We'll be driving in the dark part of the way."

Quickly Margaret Ann slipped into the back seat of the car. The seat was lumpy, but she covered it with the old blanket so she wouldn't feel the old springs so much. After stowing Henry's kit-bag into the trunk, Ted and Henry settled themselves in the front.

"Yah, well how you bin?" Henry almost shouted.

Ted was navigating the car out onto Albert Street to out of town. "Just worken and stuff," he told Henry. "Sure good that you're back."

"We're so glad to have you back, Henry," Margaret Ann was smiling now.

"Yah, well I'm damn glad to be back too," Henry began as he had already pulled out a cigarette and was lighting it.

"You gotta tell us about it," Ted now had the car out of the city, and he seemed to be relaxing a bit. Henry was offering Ted a cigarette and getting himself comfortable.

"Well let me tell you, since we have some time here on the road," Henry began, "I guess you know I joined the Air Force and first I worked as a mechanic, then I went as a test pilot and was transferred to the satellite station, and then I was put into the control tower," he paused for a only a second or so and kept on, "then from there I went overseas. They put me in with the Lancaster Bombers and then I was there.

"I got. I had a hell of a time. When I think of the food. I had pneumonia, twice, and they gave you no medication. No nothing. The only time that the doctor will look at you or put you into the hospital is if you are carried in. But you walk in. You walk right out.

"So I had a problems there. Like, so I went to my doctor, to the doctor, and I says, 'Do something with me,' because my lips were black, my tongue was white. I had patches about the size of a quarter all over my body and I had a fever like anything."

Margaret gasped, "Really," she murmured in horror.

But Henry just continued on, completely ignoring that she had made a sound. "He says, 'You know if you want to go in the hospital, you can go, but it's just as good as being in your own bed at the barracks, because we have nothing here, except extreme cases. Yes, we send them to the hospitals, but,' he says, 'what, this here of yours, you pass on will come back. But,' he says to me, 'you know what, if you want to be a fireman. There's heat all twenty-four hours a day in that place. Because the firemen, you know, they're waiting for planes coming in. You know, back and forth, or something. There's a lot of gas, there's pumps, there's everything. Now there's a bunch of guys there. It's warm there, and if you can sleep and that, I'll send you to there.'

"So he wrote me out this card, and when I went in there it was just like heaven.

"Because you had no heat in the barracks or nothing. We went to bed cold and wet. Ahh, I had a hell of a time anyway, when I went to England. It was before Christmas. So over there, the winter. We went over there and then when spring came, everything disappeared."

"What disappeared?" Ted interrupted.

"All the stuff I just said. You know, my rheumatism and just what I mentioned, disappeared. And another thing, we had was these scabies. That's another thing. Do you know what scabies are?"

Ted and Margaret Ann both said together, "No." Both were hanging on Henry's every word.

Henry went on, speaking with great authority now, "Scabies are lice . . . They hit you out here, all over. The softest parts of your system, here," he was demonstrating, his hands flying all over his body, and Margaret Ann began to be nervous that his cigarette would burn something. But he continued, "They hit you in the groins and they hit you underneath there." He was rubbing himself under his arms. "They're transparent, lice are. They go underneath the skin. They lay eggs, and everybody had them when they were over there. And that's the thing. You can't sleep with it because once you are cold. I guess they are paralyzed. When you go to bed, when you warm yourself up, then next thing you're itching so bad you can't sleep. You scratch yourself. The next morning you have blood all over your legs, everyplace, because during the night you scratch that and that thing lasts so long. And then they disappear, and you never have them again. So like in spring came, and then they put me in with the Lancasters, like with the bombers. So that was ok. And it was like that until the war ended."

Margaret Ann hated to interrupt, yet she started too, but Ted was louder than her, "So did you work on the Lancasters?"

"I worked, you see," Henry raced on with his story, "when you go to England, they put you in to different things, so many times, like that. The thing is you don't associate, because there was spies, and so forth. You know. And another things is, I don't know the real secret behind it, but even the guys that were flying the planes, like that, they would switch them around too. You made no more than two, three trips together, and they were switched again."

"Wow," Ted was all ears. Well Margaret Ann was too. They both were completely spellbound. Imagine, Henry was with the Lancasters. They had only heard of the Lancasters on the news. Imagine that.

Henry was racing on with his remembrances of the war. "The thing is, we used to joke about it. Because a guy, two guys would be fighting over a girl or something like that and they might do something on the plane, like fight or that. This is what because we used to talk about women all the time, day and night. That was our subject. We never talked about war. We never talked about where we were going. It was only women, beer and booze, and our motto was: meet them, love them, drop them," he was laughing, laughing and slapping his thighs.

Ted was laughing too, in fact hollering and laughing. "Women!" Ted was shouting.

"Yah, you bet. Women!" Henry was even louder than Ted.

In the back, Margaret Ann leaned back in the seat, trying to distance herself. Her face was stone white, and her thoughts were caught up in this revelation, women. She had never, ever, imagined Henry speaking and laughing this way about women. What did it mean?

"You too?" Ted was still laughing.

"Sure," Henry bellowed, "That was my motto too. Meet them, love them, drop them." And with that last shout he roared with laughter. "That was our motto."

Ted was still laughing, "Tell about the planes? I want to hear about the planes," he wanted to know.

Henry obliged, "I made a few trips, yah. I was second pilot, co-pilot. I made four trips. That was during the time when I wasn't sick with pneumonia.

"Then, then, before the war was ended, they put me in the control tower, and you know what a control tower is?"

"Yes," Ted wanted to hear more. In the back seat, Margaret Ann was hardly listening now. Over and over she was thinking about Henry and how proud he was of his experiences with women. All that time when she was scurrying around before work to make time to visit the church, to pray for his safety, he was thinking about women, talking about women, women, women. She sighed heavily and realized how cold she was. 'Love them, leave them,' those were the words swimming around in her head as she continued to twist the ring on her finger.

Finally she realized that Henry was still talking. "The control tower there. It was walky talky, or two way radio and then there used to be one or two guys on the truck with flares. Ground flares, and another guy in the control tower. Only time we knew when a plane was coming in and he had trouble, he had to buzz the control tower.

"Then we'd radio the guy, to give him the green flare, because the guy is coming in and he's in trouble. And then they let him in. When these planes were coming in, the guys, they were watching them and they had to come in a certain height because they can't see the runway, because it's all black-out. There was no lights of any kind and the guy would be coming in a certain depth. These guys I would watch out, how he's coming in so the plane, so that thing would be clear because it was mostly at night.

"Because we had the radar that time. We were ahead of the Americans in that war because Americans, they only bombed during the day, because they had no radar, you see. You see, when they were going over a target any plane that had a radar, the radar would show whether it was a town or it's empty. So we knew where to bomb. But the Americans hadn't no radar. So they had to bomb them by sight, during the day. So we would be coming in at night, and we would take off in the evening, about four or five o'clock in the evening. When we hit Germany it was dark, nighttime. And we had the radar. We bombed them and then we would be coming back. We would be coming back yet at night because, so we had to know how. We could come when we would. It was all signaled. It wasn't no radio or that..."

Henry was hardly stopping for a breath. He was reliving these events. "I was stationed, when we were coming back home. We would spot our station miles away because of the searchlight. We had two, three searchlights. When they crossed and one was straight up. Then when we would be going. We have information where that searchlight would be from the station, so we would know whereabouts. It would be maybe ten, fifteen, twenty, thirty miles away. But we know where our stations were, so we were heading, coming back to England, heading to the light, the searchlight. Then we spotted the searchlight, well we'd know already by compass because the guy was reading the compass. We would know where we are and then of course, when we were coming into the station, we'd circle around and then we'd come down to a certain height where we could see the flare, like the lights.

"But they were all capped and you had to be a certain level, of course, these guys that were by the entrance of the runway, they would give, if he was coming ok, everything is quiet. If he's coming different angle or something to that effect, or a different height, because he'd get a red flare that there's danger. He would take off and try it once more. But these guys if they're coming in with problems, they buzzed the tower, and we give them the preference."

Henry's voice was becoming a drone, and Margaret Ann wasn't paying attention any more. She could see the lights of their town now and their farm was only a mile on the other side.

Henry was laughing again, "Coming back to England on those flights, we always had some laughs when we finally got to the mess hall after. Always about those guys and their three point landings," he roared with laughter and jabbed Ted, "Get it, three point landings. Cause it was always about women, women, women," and he and Ted laughed.

*

Margaret Ann struggled out of the back seat without any help and joined the men who were discussing the plan that Henry would sleep in the back bedroom tonight and Ted would drive him over to his parents farm in the morning. Quietly Margaret Ann joined them and when Henry turned to her she took his hand in both of hers, then slipped quietly inside the front door.

Henry opened his hand in amazement because he felt something hard, something that Margaret Ann had left on his palm. It was the engagement ring.

Pauline

"My husband came back from the war and he got his old job back on the railroad. He was bumped from town to town, and we had to move a lot. He drank, and so I finally threw him out.

"I've never regretted going to work. Well I mean, we broke up. He was a mean drunk, and I moved out. The doctor told me if I wanted to live, I have to leave. So I had to move out. I went to work. I worked in dietary at the hospital, and I bought myself this house.

"You know if I hadn't gone to work, I don't know where I'd be. Maybe dead. You know I've got so attached to my house. It's mine, and I bought it, and I paid for it. I don't want to move. I have a large garden and a large yard. I wanted something close to work so I could walk to work. I moved in here with my son, he was sixteen. I didn't want to leave him with his father, and I didn't want him to turn into a drunk."

Anna

"My dad was born in Romania. I was born in Romania. My husband was born in Romania. We became German citizens in 1940 when the Second World War started.

"We lived through the war for five years, from 1940, but it started in 1939 already. But Hitler took us all out from Romania because we were Germans. He brought us into Germany, and we lived through the war. And then after, like I was a child through the war, like, and then when I became an adult. Like my husband, we got married and we came to Canada.

"We've been in Canada for 45 years already.

"I was a supervisor housekeeper at the hospital. The head housekeeper came to me one day, she called me in the office and she said 'I like the way you clean. You are very thorough. You know what to do. You are very efficient in your job. You're very proud of what you do, and,' she said, 'would you like to become a supervisor?' And I had so much experience, just you going to hear that.

"We had so much trouble in the housecleaning department with the supervisors, and it frightened me because they would fight all the time, and so when the head housekeeper told me this, I told her, 'I'm willing to work but when I go home, I want to leave my work and not bring it home.' She said to me, 'I promise you that as long as I'm head housekeeper, that will never ever happen because we are going to fix it.' And that's exactly what she did. She hired me and from that time we just got along beautiful. We could work with each other. We helped each other out, and before when I seen the supervisor that didn't get along. And she would come and take the furniture from the other floors. It was amazing but that's what they did.

"I just couldn't cope with that, but when I became supervisor, the head arranged it so that we all, we got along. Like when we did have a problem we talked it out the way it's suppose to be, and we still are friends today. We're retired.

"But I started to tell you about what happened in the war. When I was six years old, when the war started, Hitler took us out of Romania, 1939, because we were German. He wanted so we lived through the war. I lost my dad in the war. I lost my uncle. They were soldiers, and my cousin I lost.

"Well you see what happens when the war was on, like when Hitler took Poland in about seventeen days. Through the wartime there, and then Hitler did to us. He took us out from Romania when he took Poland in seventeen days. He took the Polish people off their farms, and he gave the farms to us. But we only stayed there until the Russians came. Like when Germany lost the war the Russians came from one end and the Americans came from the other end. So we run away from the Russians, and we ran, like just what you see on television now. The very same thing. We left everything behind. My mom took my little brother. He was three years old at the time. She took him in her arms and she hold me by the hand, and we walked for days and days until the Americans came from the front.

"You are wondering what we eat. There were still some people there in Poland. At night we would stop and the ones who were not the refugees yet, and they took us into their houses and they would give us a meal. And then the next day we would start walking again, and we was walking until the Americans came from the front.

"We was not alone. Like we just followed the traffic because there were lots of people. The people said, 'The Russians are coming. Let's get out of here.' Yes, and that's what we did.

"And then one week, the Americans did come from the front. And when they came from front, I guess then we had to quit walking and everybody put their red flags out. Like you know, we just had a stick with red on there. But that meant to the soldiers that we want peace like, you know. Nobody was shooting any more or anything. But the same thing you see on television. That's what I went through, yes. That's what I went through. It was horrible.

"All we lost everything. We lost the farm. We lost our money. Everything. Like today if there would be a war they would come like, you know, the Russians come there. They are going to hurt you. You walk out of the house and leave everything behind.

"And then we landed up in West Germany. Like East Germany belonged to the Russians. West Germany belonged to the Americans. Then when we came over the border, when we were by the Americans. The Americans were very nice to us, especially my mom because she had small children. We were all in a tent. They put us in a tent just like you see on the television today. And there were mattresses, and they gave us a white pillow, and they brought us porridge to eat. We thought we were in seventh heaven. Yes.

"It lasted from, we were moving, moving around. The war was over in May 1945, and we were on the move until 1947. We were in tents. We were in, we didn't have a house for this period of time. We were like in no-man's land or whatever you call it. But the Americans did look after us. There were lots and lots of people, just like you see on television. The same thing. There were bathrooms. The Americans put portables like. Maybe we didn't have them right from the beginning. There were no fences, no fences.

"And then in 47, then there were lots of cities, like in Germany, and the people had big houses, and they had to give up rooms for the refugees. The people who came from East Germany then and my husband was there too. How many, there were seven, eight people in one room. They lived in one room. They ate in there. They slept in there and cooked in there and baked in there. Everything. But we had a roof over our heads, and we were satisfied because we had no other choice. As the time got better United States poured money into Germany, and I guess everything was bombed down by that time. They were building up the city again and the houses again, the buildings again and the jobs. And the people got jobs again.

"My husband and I worked together.

"When I first came with my mother, I was six years old. When we lived in East Germany for what was that, 45 from until 45, and then two years we lived in no-man's land until 47 and my husband was a soldier too already by that time. And he was in, you call, in a concentration camp. But he was a prisoner. When the war was over then the Americans let all the prisoners go, and then the Red Cross found his parents. And then we had to work. My husband was on the farm. Yes, he was a farmer and that's where we met. He was twenty-three and I was sixteen.

"In Germany we got married in 1951, we were married for two years and we came to Canada and we worked on the farm.

"My husband and I worked on the farm.

"Well this is how we came to Canada. There was an article in the paper that the Canadians, that Canada looks for farm help, like to work on a farm here in Canada. We were living in one room, with our little son. We had ---- at that time. And my husband said he wanted already to go to Canada before he was married, even before he met me, but his dad didn't let him. When he applied for job his dad would rip the papers in half. His dad did.

"So when we got married, then my husband applied for job and he said, 'Dad, now you can't rip my papers, my application into half anymore because I have a family. I have to look after my family.' So my husband took the ad out of the paper, took the bus six o'clock in the morning and drove to Hannover in Germany. That's where the station was, where he had to apply to go to Canada.

"My husband walked out of the house and my father-in-law walked into our room and he said to me, 'Where's Hans?' . . . and I said . . . 'He's applying for an application. He is going to put an application in to go to Canada.' My father-in-law got so angry, but anyway he went home and my husband came back and he applied.

"The people at the application place asked all kinds of questions. Why you want to go to

Canada and he would have to give all the information, and they said they would let him know in six weeks. So after a little while we would get a letter in the mail, and we were suppose to come because you have to see all kinds of doctors and everything before they let you out of the country. So we went there, and I think we were there for a week and I have to give all my life history, and our doctors would see if you had any illnesses or anything. Then we waited for a little while, and then they told us that we were accepted.

"We packed the little stuff we had. Like clothes, we couldn't bring anything, but I had dishes and bedding and stuff, and we packed that all in big cases. And then we had to go to where the ships come in. We came in a big, big ship to Quebec. And they loaded us out and put us on a train. They had already figured out where each family goes. And we were sent to Saskatchewan, a little town called Star City and to a farmer by the name of Smith, and that's where we landed up.

"We were staying there for a month. They couldn't speak German, and we couldn't speak English, and it was terrible.

"I got so homesick and there was a Mister Brown, here in Saskatoon who looked after all the immigrants. And the farmer said, like my husband, he was a good farmer. My husband could drive a tractor and he had his license in Germany and everything. So there was no problem there. But I was the problem because all I could see was sky and the clouds and the sun and land all around you. That's how big the farm was. There was nothing else. There was a farm in the middle and that's all I seen day after day after day.

"My husband went out in the fields, and we had a little house. I lost so much weight and I couldn't eat any more. I could cook for myself. I would take a piece of bread, and I would chew and chew and chew but it wouldn't go down. And I lost so much weight. I always was very thin when I was young, but . . . The farmer he could see that, so he phoned and got in touch with Mister Brown from Saskatoon, and the farmer told him, 'I haven't got anything against this German family, but if the lady has to stay, she is going to die because she can't eat.'

"So then they, Mister Brown from Saskatoon, he put us out to the Mennonite farms. They spoke German. So we went there to the Mennonite church. I could speak and they teach me how to bake bread and cookies. I was eighteen years, and then we stayed at that

Mennonite farm until our son had to go to school. But we didn't have a vehicle at the time so that meant someone had to drive him to school every day, a country school.

"Then the farmer said to my husband, that he didn't have a trade, and he said maybe Hans should move to the city and look for something else. So we did and my husband went to the unemployment office in Saskatoon and there were lots of jobs, but all farmer jobs.

"When we came from Germany, we had to come as immigration, that we were going to stay a year on the farm, because we owed them $500 for bringing us over. And we made the money, and we paid off that money. I'm telling you, every dollar we saved and we would go and pay off so that we would get rid of this $500 debt we had.

"By that time my husband bought a truck, a second hand truck and we moved to Saskatoon. We rented a little suite on Avenue D. By that time I had a second child already, and Hans went to the unemployment office. And they wanted to put us back on the farm again. And he said, 'I don't want to go back on the farm.' And well they said, 'We don't have nothing else.' But he would go there every day, and at that time we met somebody already who could speak

German. And one day he went in there and they said, 'We don't have nothing, but I want you to come back tomorrow again.'

"So the next day he went there again. And the guy said, 'You know they are building City Hospital, and they need men on construction. They need somebody who pushes sand on construction.' And my husband says, 'I'll take anything as long as it's a job.' But the guy says, 'It's only for three days. That's all they need you.'

"My husband said, 'Well that's better than nothing.' He started, and he was never unemployed until he got ill. He worked, and later on he learned the trade to become a tile-setter. He worked as a tile-setter until he retired and got sick. And I worked at the hospital.

"Well when I came to Canada, I wasn't expecting a lot. All I wanted, my goal was, if I have a little house with a white little fence and a car. That was enough for me. I was never reaching to have a lot. I have support, my family, my friends, and my church, and my faith, and my prayer, and God."

Elizabeth

"I was born in England in a little village. In England we knew that the war was coming years before it did, and so there was a huge recruitment. I joined the British Red Cross at sixteen years, and I trained for three years for war, not for hospital work or anything like that, for ambulance driving and getting people out of bombed buildings all that kind of thing.

"You can't say you liked war, but there was certain excitement about it because we were bombed regularly. I was in the Battle of Britain in the blitz and from then, I just went on.

"So I was sixteen when I joined the British Red Cross. I was born in 1920. So, in 1939, you see I couldn't, although I joined when I was sixteen years old, I wasn't a full member until I was nineteen. But those three years I was training for war. So when war was declared, we were in it straight away.

"And where I lived, which was twenty-nine miles south of London, the Germans had three lanes to go over to bomb London. So we were very near, and we lived under the middle lane. So we were bombed on a regular basis, and not only that, there were the flights over head, the bombers were coming over and aircraft were intercepting them, and trying to, you know, shoot them down. And so, and at the same time the men were being called up, and so we have to take over from the men, and we had to drive ambulances. We were in the first-aid posts. We had to do everything as it came along because we didn't know what was happening.

"My family got bombed. The roof was blown off three times and nobody was hurt. I had a brother who was in the war, but the others weren't old enough.

"When I look back it's more terrifying actually. The different incidences then . . . It was then . . . , but everybody was in it, you know.

"We had mansions, that of course we never went into when it was peace time because of the class, you know. They were the top class. But when war came, they opened up their whole mansions, and we had our first aid posts in the mansions. And we had, you know, . . . Everybody was on one level then. Which was rather nice. Distinction, that was the word I was looking for, there was class distinction before the war, but it came back immediately after the war. But during the war they were no different than we were. They were helping us just as much, you know.

And everybody gave up their cars, you know, to get the people to the hospital. And their vans were the ambulances, and everything was on a nice level.

"After the war I continued in training for a nurse. Then I got married. I met my husband. He was from the next village. I think it must have been at a dance that I met him, or something. I can't really remember. We had two daughters and then my husband died when my girls were thirteen and fourteen, and we came to Canada.

"My husband died of a heart attack. The reason I came to Canada was because I had a brother living in Canada, and he just lost his wife and he had two daughters. And so we decided it would be a good idea to come to Canada and help each other. Which we did. My brother lived in Saskatoon.

"I worked in a nursing home, immediately I got here. I think I had a job within three days. My credentials for nursing that I brought, which weren't sufficient as an RN. And so I worked in a nursing home, and then I worked in city hospital and from there I took more training and I worked there for the remaining of the 60's and 70's.

"And, then stupid me, I remarried, and I haven't been nursing since.

"His wife was a patient in the hospital. I became quite friendly with her, and she was in and had a lot of cancer and then she died. That's when I met that skunk. So after I wised up and left that man. Then I went to BC to Queen Charlotte city.

"You know on Queen Charlotte Island, and they have a little hospital there. But they didn't have any vacancies, so I worked in a hardware store until I retired.

"I finally divorced my second husband, and moved back here to Saskatoon to be close to my family."

Patrick

"When I come out of school, during the Second World War, I joined the Navy, come back and got discharged and went to school a little bit. Then went to work on construction and got laid off and needed a job.

"Oh, you want more!! OK, I tell you.

"Well I was born on a farm, and I was five years old when we moved off. My dad died in an accident. I had three older sisters and two younger sisters. So here was mom left with all these children.

"Well I joined the Navy in 43. It was forced on you. It was society pushed it on you. Well if you were growing up and stuff and were walking around and you looked healthy. That's the way society was, you know. So you just had to go whether you liked it or not.

"So I joined the Navy.

"Well because I didn't like so much marching. I was lazy. I tried to get in the Air Force first, and my eyesight didn't allow it. There was the first building downtown there. The Air Force said it's their recruiting stations for reasons in the Air Force. Well, they said, 'Well you go and take this here paper to that place downstairs.' Pretty near shoved me in the Army.

"I walked from there down to the Navy. I was mad enough to do that. Well I was, and I was off. I went to Newfoundland. At that time, it wasn't Canada. But I was discharged in 45.

"In the Navy it's different than going overseas. You don't go to the action. So you're involved different, around the port and so on. Around the country in the ocean. So I was discharged in 45.

"Yeah, I went to TVS up there. I didn't complete my grade 12, and I went up to finish, and so I planned on going into university . . . I planned on going into university, but I had used up too many of my credits and stuff.

"So then I met her, well met her again. We grew up in the same town. Our folks knew each other for years and years."

He was looking over at his wife now, who was sitting patiently beside him, a quiet little woman, who was quick to smile.

"Our grandfathers, my grandfathers and her grandfathers on her mother side all came up here together from some place in the States to homestead.

"I was going to go into Civil Engineering, but then . . . Then I got a job with a trucking company. Then I went down to McGavin's Bakery and got a job. I was thirty-eight years driving a truck. I was foreman for nine years. Then I was on the country trucks. I think there was one territory. I went to Rosetown, Elrose, Eatonia and back to Kindersley and back and then the next day go down through Dinsmore, Beechy, Lucky Lake and then repeat it again on the second day.

"Then I found out I had diabetes ins'ipidus."

[Diabetes insip'idus is: "a metabolic disorder resulting from decreased activity of the posterior lobe of the pituitary gland. Reabsorption of water from the renal tubules is promoted by vasopressin, or antidiuretic hormone, a hormone from the posterior pituitary lobe. A deficiency of this hormone leads to the symptoms of diabetes insip'idus which include excessive thirst and passage of excessive amounts of urine with no excess of sugar." Miller, B. F., & Keane, C. B. (1972). *Encyclopedia and Dictionary of Medicine and Nursing*, Philadelphia: W. B. Saunders Co.]

"I was tired on the job. I think I was born tired. They found out I had cancer. I guess the wife realized I just couldn't do my job. I'd come home at ten o'clock at night, and I was supposed to be at home by six. Then I was supposed to go again in the morning, and they were going to fire me. But the wife, she phoned to my doctor and went to see him that afternoon and got a letter. The letter said, it should be my last day of work. I was on eleven medications by that time. I had these black outs. It wasn't a stroke or nothing. I wouldn't know where I was.

"So here I am. She looks after me."

They were looking at each other, holding hands. A very tender moment. Then he continued, "All my life it was money that I lacked. The main thing is money. You're hungry. You got to eat.

"Money, I mean. I didn't have a choice to go to university. I was at a crossroads.

"Yeah, I guess I could have gone for more schooling, but that would have meant going into debt.

"I think the one thing too that happened to me, to a lot of people my age. We were brought up during the depression where security wasn't very good, and then we got into the war. And I think this is an overbearing that you had to have security afterwards. Maybe you wouldn't take a chance, and this type of thing, but I think this has been a negative thing for me, Lack of security, not wanting to take a chance. That would have been too big a risk. I mean more than money by that. I mean security, security for life, security for your friends, for your family.

"Security, I mean, I may be wrong in saying this, but I don't know, this is my feeling anyway."

Bernadette

"We were so poor, we never see the doctor too often, you know. Maybe I remember in all my life once the doctor. So we get this Métis woman. She was a native. She has all kinds of herbs and potions, and she was making. And like she would send my father in the spring into the woods to get specific things for the stomachache or . . . and he would use it. The things they were more like roots to pick out, some kind of roots of the herbs. Some kind of edible stuff. It was like a string looking but it was just at the foot of a tree. Sometimes they could find it. I know the syrup she take. I don't know if I can say it in English. It was some kind of a seed. After you boil it, it gets really runny, and she put some sugar and other stuff in it, and it was good. Because if you have sore throat, it helped. It just go down like Jell-O. But it was thicker then syrup.

"My father was French and my mother was Métis. My father's family, my brother traced it, and I think it goes back to France in about 1500 or 1600 something. They first came with the French in Quebec.

"I worked for ten years after I got married. When I was younger, in Montreal, I worked in a hospital and after that when I got married I worked for a store.

"I grow up in Quebec. There were nine of us in the family. I was the second youngest and I had one brother younger, than I. I went to school until ten, when we moved north of Quebec where my father died. Actually he had an accident. Then I quit school and I just worked to help my mother. When I was eighteen years, I went to Montreal because all my brother was there, eh. So we were living at one of my brother when my mom got sick. She died two years after my father.

"Then I got married, in the 50's. He came to Montreal when I was there. He went into the army. He was shipped to Korea. So he went to Korea, and when he come back we got married. My husband got out of the army and worked for the base. There was an opening for a qualified mechanic, and he got the job. So they were sending people all over, other than the base near Montreal. Those you want to go, so we said yes sure, we'd take a transfer because like me we didn't have, we were not big schooling. We didn't have it. Neither of us. But for working in a store, I could do that. Like it was a good job. It was not big money, but it was a job. It was a steady job. So we went. So we went to Alaska. We lived four years in Alaska. And they close the base. Then they transfer us to Dundurn. We didn't stay in Dundurn. We lived in the city.

"My husband had manic depression. It started when he got back. The war I mean. But he always came back from the depression fast, you know. He was a mood swing all the time, up and down, but it really got bad after. Not because of my father-in-law it was just that he was getting older. I guess, and the disease just got worse with my husband, and he never wanted to get some help. Saying that . . . was difficult you know. He was not violent. He never hit me, or things like that. But he was just like, oh, it was indescribable. They get all the good and all the bad you know. They can be so wide in everything they do. They can go. Everything is fine. They're high, very happy. They don't see nothing wrong. They can buy lots of stuff and everything is good. But when they see it. They put it worse than it is. They go really depressed. You never know what day. What they are going to be the next. You never know.

"Around 76, 77, he finally went to see the doctor. The doctor put him on anti-depression, because he was very bad. But when he started getting better, he went wild, because he quit the pills. And then he went up, you know what I mean. Those people who got those disease really like it, when they are high because everything is so beautiful for them. But what they don't like is the depression. And the more my husband was doing depression, the deeper he got, every time. So finally I had to come and see my doctor and told my husband the next day about the pills, what the pills can do for him and can keep him from those deep depression.

"But one day we pulled in here, and he was starting in depression and went so deep. He was in the bedroom for weeks. Didn't want to come out. Didn't want to see any friend. People were coming, like his old friend was coming to see him. Didn't want to see them.

"My husband has never been really happy.

"He died seven years ago. Yes, it's going to be seven years in the fall. Nothing to do with his sickness. He died in his bed from an aneurysm. He was a young man, forty-five years. Forty-five is not old.

"He actually worked all through this. When he was in depression, he didn't work, but he never took holiday or sick leave, all that many years. He could take off, eh, so when he was in those depression, he didn't work. He had so much sick leave time.

"I don't know how I was holding it together. I don't know. It's because I always, I never let myself go depressed. That's something I didn't want for myself. So I never look at the bad side of things. I always tried to look at the, anything that was on the bright side. I was looking at it. If it meant going out at midnight and sit and look at the stars, I will do it if that could help me. You know, what I mean. I never let that put me down.

"A lot of people tell me, divorce him, because I know that not every people can take care of people that are manic depression. They take their family for strangers and strangers for their family, and that's true. . .

"He couldn't get any help otherwise and he knew I'm the only one that could help him. I know that I can help him, and so I stay.

"When I think of my life, I really think that I am pretty lucky. I think I have been pretty lucky in my life, because I have my health, and I was always able to deal with all those kinds of stuff, that come my way, without falling apart. For me I think that's a good thing. That's a big thing."

Louise

"My mother died when I was 12 years old. I was born in Holland. Well to begin, when my mother died, then my dad got married again, and I couldn't get along with my stepmother. Then my dad ended up in a concentration camp during the war. My mother died of pneumonia and it turned into TB, and then she go to a sanitarium, but my dad was running around with a young girl. So my mom thought if she went to a sanitarium my dad, you know, my dad would have free sailing. My mother thought she should stayed home because she was always in bed, always resting in the front room. I remember.

"Then later when my mother died. My dad married this young girl, and I always blame her for my mother's death. She was five years older than me, twenty-five years younger than my dad. They were working together. So she was kind of a little girl. My dad was a printer like for the government, like printing maps for the army. So he had a great big machine, and he had some girls working with him. You know, to keep the machines clean. She was one of them. When the war broke out my father wound up in a concentration camp. I was with the neighbors, and then I was with an aunt and then I was with a friend.

"Well my dad, he had pictures in his pocket. They found out from . . . oh, I don't know exactly, and he was with the underground. So he got picked up. He was found with pictures, and it was a long story, pictures of Germans coming out of the airplanes, you know.

"Well this girl and him weren't married yet, but then they got married when my dad came out of concentration camp. So she was with us. She stayed with us but she went home to her mom and dad. So I was alone in the house. So then I went with the neighbors and I was a waif of the government and we were under the Germans. So I was kind of under the German regime. So I had to go every month to a lady to tell them how my work was in the school, this and that.

"I was going to school and then well my food was hard to get, so I was with neighbors and when the food ran out they said go some place else, you know. So I stayed with an aunt, and I stayed with a girl friend and all over the place. I was an only child, so . . .

"And when I came here to Canada, I think, I started eating. And when the kids left something on their plate. I would eat it myself. I would never throw it away you know, because we never had no food during the war.

"But let me go on telling you about in Germany, my step mother, I kind of blamed her for my mother's death. If my mother had went to the sanitarium, she might have got better, but my mother wouldn't leave the house because she thought that girl would move in and dad would have free sailing. And while my mom was at home, well she kind of protected me. She knew what was going on with me.

"My dad was kind of a tyrant. He was. He hit me a lot and he always hit me in my face with his fist. And then I go like this, and he would hit my shoulder, you know. He was always after me, you know, and this and that. He was a mean guy. He came here, when he retired, and then he got a divorce from that woman because she started running around with a younger guy. They got a divorce and then he came here because he wanted to see his grandchildren grow up. Like I was the only child at home so I had the only grandchildren. So he came here and he died here. He was with us for four and a half years, but he was mean to my kids. You know, because I was working then and he was kind of alone with them at times. I don't know. He was just a mean person.

"But I want to tell you about meeting my husband. That's a long story too. My mother, when she was young, she was working for the English Consul. And he was in Holland six months and in England six months. My mother, she was working then and then the World War One broke out. And she was kind of a babysitter, a nanny. She helped in the kitchen. She was in housekeeping. So she went with this family, and they went to England and then the World War One broke out. So they couldn't get back to Holland.

"So she met a lot of friends in England, you know. She met the other nannies there and one of these people that she knew from the World War One, she got married to a Canadian. And then when the Canadians came to Holland in

World War Two, well they said, 'See if these people are still alive because we couldn't write to them.' So this Canadian came to the house with this letter from this English person.

"And then him and me was going out, and he brought friends and you know all that. And my husband, to be, was one of the friends. It's kind of a long crazy story. So I met my husband that way then. Well I met him on June 9 exactly, and then they had to go back in November.

"And when the war was over, and then he says, 'Will you come with me.'

"I said, 'No, I don't love you.'

"I was just, I learned English in school. So I could talk with him a little bit, but I was shy. And then but my dad and his wife, I couldn't get along with them. The country was in chaos, you know like during the war. So I thought well that was my way out. I know I didn't love my husband then but I kind of learned to love him, you know.

"When I was here, because I was going to write a book about my life, cause the kids always said write a book and, and I didn't, but I put it on tape, through old letters and through research and all that. And I got it on tape, and I got to know myself a lot through telling about my life, you know. I learned a lot and I thought.

"I came to Canada. He came in January, and I didn't come until September. I wait and so, I thought, it was a way out, to get out of there, and I didn't know what I was getting into.

"But he was so good. He was always helping me. We came to the prairies to Saskatoon and lived with his mother and his father. I learned a lot from her. They were nice people from what I could understand. At first I couldn't understand them very good. You know it was kind of a crazy time, but I were young. I was nineteen or twenty then. Like, I was very adventurous, and I like came through the war by myself and I thought I will just stick up for myself.

"I started a new life. It turned out good. I've never been sorry.

"My husband's family were Polish, but they were good people and my husband was a good person. He helped me a lot because when I came here I spoke like, well you learn English in school, you know, like the Queen speaks that high English. And he hated it. And he said you're in Canada. Now speak like a Canadian. And when I said something in English, he said, 'Say it this way.' He was always correcting me but it helped.

"He was kind. He wasn't like my dad. My dad would hit me, but my husband was very good, very patient, everything you know, when we had kids too. He was always playing with the kids on the floor. Very patient and they all loved their dad.

"But you know, he died when he was 55 and I was 51. You know, he couldn't take civilian life, you know, and then he joined the Air Force after about five or six years. Then he was stationed here, and then he was posted in France, like with the advance party through NATO. I was happy to go to France. So I would go to Holland. We lived in France for three and a half years. I went to Holland to visit friends and neighbors and all that, but not for my dad, you know. He was kind of mean. I don't know, I couldn't stand him, you know.

"We came back here and because in France there was so much drinking going on, and my husband said, 'That's no place to raise kids.' And we had my youngest son was born when we lived in France. No, he was born in Germany because there was complications and all that. Then we had another one born when we came to Canada. So we have 5 kids there, you know. And he said that was no place to raise kids in the Air Force. So much drinking, so many parties, and so he got out when his five years was up.

"Then we came back to Saskatoon because that was home town for him. Then we lived with his mother for a while until we got a house here. And then we were on our own. He worked with the school board. He was kind of maintenance with the school board. Well he wasn't making much money, and then I was twenty-eight years at the veteran-home housekeeping.

"My husband died of a heart attack. He died in his sleep.

"I felt so sorry for myself. I thought, 'I came to this country and what for,' all that. And Joe always says, 'I'll be there for you,' and I thought, 'Now that I need you the most where are you?' I felt sorry for myself. And the kids, they saw that, and they kind of pushed me through it. They made me become independent. I started to learn how to drive a car.

"When I think back on my life, I guess it was survival, like. I was very selfish then. I was more looking for myself, but I came to love, and then I got kids. First I didn't like kids, and then when they are your own, you got to love them, you know. You got to love them, you know, you got to love them. And you got to look after then. I took it day by day, I guess. I wasn't making plans for the future or anything.

"When Joe died, well the kids told me, 'You know, you're on your own now. You've got to learn to live for you.' And it took me quite a while because I was banking on them all the time you know.

"The youngest daughter was at home, and I thought she would stay at home with me, but she had a boy friend. And she was going out, and she drove the car. She would drop me someplace, like at a friend's place, and so she would drop me off and then pick me up later. I thought she would take over for her dad, but she didn't. She said, 'I've got to live my own life.'

"So I would think, 'What would Joe do,' you know. And I still think that, you know. You've got to make a decision. What would he do, you know? It still come in my mind, eh, after all these years."

Russell

"I was a firefighter. That was my occupation in my life before I retired, but I was an air gunner during the war and we had ten, twelve hours a flight. And I think my arthritis came from then. Like we had no heat in the billets, and we only had blankets and everything was kind of damp down in the barracks. And when you were a gunner, you always sat in that cramped position in the plane.

"Well to begin with, I come through the depression when nobody had any money. I was born in Saskatoon, and then we went to a farm. I was two or three years old. I was on the farm until I was in the service.

"I met her over there, in England. We got married over there during the war. And we had a boy then, and I think she was pregnant with the second.

"I was in the war, being a gunner. It was very cold. Well, I was in coastal command, and we did 800 hours for a tour in the Bay of Biscay. That's where the coldness comes. Like you know, well the billets didn't have coal. The blankets were kind of damp, so that's where I thought I got arthritis and they wouldn't believe it over there. I remember I was in the hospital once, for a cold or flu or whatever.

"But then I was really very fortunate when I really was in heavy action. I mean I was very fortunate to get back to her. I mean home.

"We were in the bay so it was coastal command, not as bad as a bomber, I guess, but I flew twelve trips with one crew, and then this guy said, he would take my place on the next flight. I was on the same station as him. He didn't make it back.

"When I came home to Saskatoon after the war, I was going to be an electrician, and then the guy didn't come through with the deal. Like so, I thought well this would be . . . like there was an advertisement in the paper that said for veterans to apply to the fire department or police department and we thought well we'd have a wage and at the end we'd have a pension and we, well that's the main reason. I thought, well it would be a steady job being a fireman.

*

"When we were leaving England, her mother didn't want her to come. She tried to pull her off the train."

*

Russell's wife added this:

"My mom died a year later, so yes, I was homesick. I had brothers and sisters back in England, and this was a different country I came to. I was lucky. Russell's mom and dad were English. They had come over from England. So it wasn't like I married into a different nationality. My mother in law was good at showing me how to cook. So I was lucky."

Lara

"I was born in Austria, but during the war in 1939, in 37 I went to England and stayed there until 1946. In the 30's, jobs were hard to get. But I was a companion living in England.

"So when the war came, I was about nineteen. I was born in 1914. The war came in 1939 wasn't it? I was born in Austria, Nobody sent me to England. I went on a holiday to England.

"Just about that time was the time when the Nazi's were very active in Germany, and they were also starting to go into Austria. I wanted, I always wanted to travel in the younger days. We didn't have much money, and dad, well travelling was out because there were no airplanes that you could afford. There were no buses. There was nothing. So the first I said to my family, 'I would like to go to England on my holiday.'

So I went to England on my holiday, which was an experience as well, but I took the train to Germany, to Belgium and to England. And then when I was there the Austrian Embassy and the Austrian hostel, I stayed there first for my holiday. I booked in there. And after I got there my father wrote me a letter, and he said to me, 'If you can stay in England, please stay,' he said. 'Don't come back,' he said, 'because it's terrible here,' he said. They arrested him a few times. The Nazi's did, because and so on, and he said, 'Stay in England if you can.'

"I was just a tourist you know. So I got to know a lady, that lady that I was working for then. She spoke several languages, and I met her, and she said, 'Why don't you come to be my companion and work for me.' She says that, and that would be an excuse for the English government would let me stay there, you know. So I did and she had higher connections, you know. So I was never interrogated, which was very good because most of the allies were interrogated, and I stayed there until I met my husband there in England.

"I tell you more about what happened to my family. There they were stayed in Austria. My father was arrested a few times for treason. They were, well they were, Hitler of course was there, you know. That's the only way they couldn't touch dad because they had nothing on him really, you know.

"My sisters were both teachers and my youngest sister, her father-in-law, he was a principal in a school. And the Nazi's gave orders for them to teach the doctrine. And he refused in a way, not saying to them, just give the teaching that's all there was there, you know. In those days, so many people like teachers and students they became all Nazi's you know, in Austria there. And they checked on them all the time. It wasn't whether they didn't teach that doctrine, you know, as much as you should know it. And one day he didn't come back from work. They found him shot on a kind of crossroads. They found him shot.

"That was one of the incidents that hit our family close. There was so many other instances that was just terrible. I wasn't there, but the family found that as long as Hitler was there, there was at least enough to eat. My mother grew a big garden of course, always did, you know.

"When Hitler was defeated, there was a spell when there was nobody there and the food was so skimpy. They ground up (a German word) . . . to make coffee, you know, and this sort of thing.

"Then the English occupied part of the country where my family lived. Austria was occupied by the Russians around Vienna, and the French on west side and the English on the south side. And the English occupation, and my father was there, he was so angry that my mother started smoking. She was grieving for . . . and my father went every day to the market, you know. A guy came in and this sort of thing, and they were all English occupation troops, you know. And they, my family, asked one of the young soldiers to come for coffee one day. One of the guys, one of the English soldiers and my mother made the best cake and coffee she could make, and she had flowers and a basket full of whatever, biscuits or whatever she made and this sort of thing. Well the man thanked them very much and three days later he came to the house, and he brought a whole bag of food for then. Beef, bread, and a little bag of margarine and my father, they all, just thought it was heaven. My sister told me all that. I wasn't home.

"She told me. My mother made a cake and invited him you know, and he was so happy to have that, and that guy brought occasionally some food for them to eat until things got better.

"This sort of thing but there are lots of other stories, like my sister she was a teacher and they sent her to Yugoslavia to teach. She spoke Yugoslavian, the language. And she had to teach down there. But they were in the German building. Everything was Germanized you know. So when she got to the village, she was supposed to teach the children. The people were very, very afraid of her because they were thinking she was a Nazi and all the rest of it. And after about six months, they found out she wasn't.

"And my mother and father went down one Christmas to spend it with her, and of course they took some food packets. They were all farmers where my sister was teaching, and mother and father went down. On Christmas morning, my sister found all baskets of food and stuff by her door that the farmers brought in, you know. And eggs and chicken and ham and all this. And she didn't know where it was coming from. And a little boy comes with a basket, and he said, 'We want to give you this, teacher, for your mom and dad to take it home to Austria.' It was so nice. It was so sad. So much crying with that, you know.

"And there was a few other stories of course. And my youngest sister she was a teacher. She had to join Hitler youth. They had to work on farms and stuff like that you know, and to be enrolled in the army, you know. And she was. She escaped there, and she went to my sister's in Yugoslavia to hide there. And she was hiding there of course, you know.

"And then there was the time when there was such torment between the Nazis and Yugoslavia. They had the home groups were starting to fight you know, making it kind of. . . And the French were doing the same, and then they were fleeing Yugoslavia, both of them, my sisters, over the mountains, over the Alps. And they run into Nazi and of course you are welcome. They were leave everything and in one of those camps, my sister played the harmonica and my other sister played the guitar you know. So they were playing music for them. They wanted music, the Nazi's did. So they played for them. And Maria said, 'We played almost all night, and when they fell asleep, we walked down the mountain. And we were traveling day and night to get away from them.'

"And so they get on the Austria side and you know, the Yugoslavian, Austria side, and then they run into some English there. And the English, Maria she demanded they wanted to see the captain, you know. She told the whole story and their captain, the English captain was nice to her. The next troop transport that came from Filla, the truck you know, they gave them passage on their truck to go back home. But then they had to get off because the English were going another way, and they were standing at the crossroad. But they stood there for a whole day, before one of the soldiers took pity on them and took them to my hometown where they lived.

"There were so many stories that can be told. I didn't see all that. I was in England.

"Well they survived the war. Only one that died was my sister's father-in-law, like the one that was shot.

"They had it hard. I had it better in England. We got rations, you know, two slices of bacon and two ounces of sugar a week, you know. We could manage those things, you know, and then of course we had cars too. I wasn't too badly off in England. No we always had something to eat, you know.

"I met my husband. He was a Canadian. I met him at a dance. There were lots of dances taking place, and they asked us ladies, girls, to dance you know. The different associations had the dances, and so we went, and that's how I met him. We married there in England, and my first daughter was born there. And then I came as a war bride over to Canada.

"First I came to the farm where his family lived, you know, in Saskatchewan. And we didn't know what we're going to do then because he was very shell shocked. His nerves were bad, but he did manage to work a little bit. So from there we came off the farm. Then his father died, when we lived in Melfort and we came to Saskatoon and we settled down eventually.

"And of course he was sick a lot. He was under doctor's care all the time. We had two children. My children were good to me. I was working hard all the time you know, morning till night and then at home. I borrowed money for their education, and they paid it back to me after.

"My husband was an alcoholic besides. Yes, it was difficult. Yes, I'm so glad, I was strong. I come from a very sturdy family. Sometimes, it was better at times, you know, and then. It would be better and the next time, you know, and it kept me going again, you know. Then my husband died in 1984. He never worked much before he died. I had to look after him, but his mind was very, very disorganized, very bad. I think it all started with the war. He was and drinking, that didn't help, unfortunately.

"When we came here, his family, they were so shocked when he came back. I mean he was drinking in England. I remember that, but it was normal for all the soldiers, you know. And anyway the story was they were making bombs out and the bridge, well it . . . and the Germans surprised them, and he was shooting at everything that was in sight. And the sergeant had to hit him over the head to knock him completely out because he didn't know what he was doing any more and . . .

"He was a nervous person to begin with. He should never have joined the army, but they didn't select them very carefully. In those days every one had to go into the army to fight the war.

"I shouldn't say it, but I was very relieved when he died, because it . . . This is a world that is over now.

"Now my kids are very good to me. I try to see my life as an adventure. I think you learn all the time. There's always things new that you learn.

*

"When I was in England, I got a letter from the German embassy that I had to leave at a certain time and I had to be back to my homeland or the fatherland as they called it, you know. Well I packed my trunk and then that lady came, and she said, 'You know you shouldn't go.' She said, 'You should stay,' she said. I already had my mind made up. I was going to stay. But then when that letter came from the embassy, I thought, 'I may never see my homeland again,' but I said, 'No, I'm not going to go and that's it.' But I had to make a decision too. There was only a day between when the embassy told me to come back, you know. I never went of course.

"I heard so many stories. I may never see my family again, you know, but then I was told after that, that another girl hated that letter from the German embassy to go, but she left and she never got home. She disappeared in Germany. The family never heard from her. So that was a sign for me that I was really lucky that I didn't go home at that time, you know. It was the right decision."

Hildegarde

"I was nineteen years old, and I went to help out in the war. I lived in Holland. I was in nurse training at the time, and it got interrupted by the invasion. So I went into the Red Cross. I was in my second year of nursing. Everything stopped with the invasion. We were sent to the Red Cross. We got phoned to volunteer there.

"So like I said, I didn't last long. The first week of duty, and the trouble was I got wounded on my day off.

"It was my day off and I had some things to do at home. So I took a day off and I went home to wash clothes. I was kind of cleaning all that up, you know and that's when I got wounded. Well not right there at home but . . .

"You see we lived right on the front line, where I lived. It was pretty scary. We had bomb shelters, but it was no use, because you go to a shelter and they bomb a shelter. You know, you go in your basement or something, but my house never got bombed.

"Oh, there were signals. Like that, there would be an air raid siren go off. But mostly, you just hear the aircraft coming, and that's it, that was it. On the front line you don't hear the sirens or anything. They just shoot whenever they feel like it. Back and forth, back and forth, and that's why we ran out right in the front line. We nurses had to pick up the ones who were shot, help them.

"We had all kinds of soldiers there. We had Americans, Canadians, English, French, Dutch. They all come to that front line and take the turn to go and fight you know, and come back again.

"My house was right there on the river there, and across the river that's where the big battle was. It was Nijmegen Island, in 1944. I lived there from 1940 until 1951 when I came to Canada.

[Nijmegen, Nijmegen Bridge is part of a major battle called 'Operation Market Garden.']

"I came to Canada with my first husband. Well, we don't talk about him very often any more. My husband here, this guy." And she pointed to her husband who was sitting beside her. "He knows him very well."

And her husband smiles and nods his head several times, and says an exaggerated, "Oh yes."

"I got married in Holland. My first husband was a brother of my best girl friend. But I divorced my first husband. I met him," and she takes her husband's hand, "when I came to Canada. He was a boarder. He lived with us, and, and he came from Saskatchewan, and he worked in Ontario at the time. Well we seemed to click. My first husband was an alcoholic."

"She lost her leg in the war," her husband spoke quietly.

Hildegarde went on, "I have an artificial leg. Well my leg was shot off in World War Two, in Holland. You see I was called back to work because of the shelling, and I was shot. A mortar shell. My friend he was with me, and he got killed. I lost my leg. There were three of us, my friend was in front and I was second and the old fellow was in the back."

The husband quickly took over, "They were running for shelter. They got the young fellow in front, in the chest, and got her in her belly and her leg. The old fart behind got nothing, and he run like hell, and left her lying there."

"Yes," Hildegarde continued, "Yes, he left both of us lying there. Now it was dangerous but there was another man later on, I found out, it was a minister, he came up to us. And he sat between me and my friend because I didn't realize then. I was going to... I was going to pull myself up to my friend, to see if I could help him, but I couldn't stand up. But this minister, he went in-between us because he could see that my friend was dead already. Because his whole face was gone, and this minister, he sat between us and he sat with me until they came to give me first aid. It was night already when they finally could come to me. He, the minister, sat with me for four hours there until they finally took me to the hospital and I've never been able to find out who he was. But somebody who saw it said it was a minister. I tried and tried, but he never would come forward.

"So then I had my ride looking at the sky." She laughs, "They took me up in the jeep, like sideways like that on the stretcher. You see sometimes, you remember, you know somebody on the stretcher."

She was demonstrating with her arms, throwing her head sideways, "Well I was one of those, and they laid me this way over the jeep so I could see the shells come over, houses burning, and I could see everything was broken, no windows. I think I was in shock. I didn't feel nothing. They gave me first aid. They just tied it together with bandages. They also gave me a shot. I think it was morphine or something. Four days later I came out of my coma. And I had this stump, a middle stump and my belly was cut open, I don't know the name of the operation, but I have a great big scar.

"Later on my dad bought me a little motor scooter, two wheels with motor on the front. They made me a new artificial leg here in Canada."

How fortunate for Hildegarde that she met this young man from Saskatchewan, who became her second husband. His trade was carpentry, and when they made their home in Saskatoon, he built her kitchen cupboards, stove, and sink, plus bathroom cupboards and sink, to a convenient height so she manages very well in their home. She was in a wheel chair.

"Let me tell you a bit about my life in Holland, before that day when I was shot," she began again, "My dad, he married again, and he and his wife didn't want me. I had to beg for my food from the neighbors when I was young. I guess that's why I married so young. I was half starved. I smoked a lot then too. The Canadians gave me cigarettes.

"My dad died in a concentration camp in Germany. They didn't take me, or my mom, just my dad. He was a Jew. Yes, all Jews were taken. I was lucky that my mom was married to a Christian. Like my stepfather was a Christian, but my dad went with his wife and two kids. They never came back. So that was it. It was a tough life, but you got to learn to live with it. There's no use crying over spilt milk. Yahh.

"My first husband. He came to Holland during the war. He came in the Canadian army, and he was stationed in Germany after the war. After I divorced him he sent me letters once in a while, Yahh. I just threw them in the fire. I wanted nothing to do with him. I was too young to be married, too starved, too scared. I was married too very young. I was 19 at the time.

Then she and her husband stole a glance, "Now I think of my life it's sort of like that song, 'The Green, Green Grass of Home.' I'm home now in Saskatchewan."

About the Author

MURIEL MONTBRIAND is a retired Associate Professor (Nursing) and Research Associate, Applied Research/Psychiatry, University of Saskatchewan, Canada. A Registered Nurse (Reg.N), she received her Doctor of Philosophy (Ph D) under the Department of Psychiatry, College of Medicine, University of Saskatchewan. Saskatoon, Saskatchewan in 1994. She retired in 2005.

During her academic career she received 16 professional awards. Two of these awards were international awards specifically for writing:

- the Susan Baird Excellence in Writing Award in Clinical Practice - 2000, *Oncology Nursing Forum* Twenty-fifth Annual Congress, San Antonio, Texas, and

- the 1995 Award for the Best Original Research Paper in Cancer Nursing, *Cancer Nursing*, Lippincott - Raven Publishers.

As a socio-health researcher, her expertise was and continues to be the use of herbs and natural products, plus the ways people tell their life-stories.

ALSO BY MURIEL J. MONTBRIAND

FICTION

Murders at Macabre Cove

NONFICTION

Memories of My Dad
(private publication)

Sunshine Sketches of the Summerplace
(private publiation)

ACADEMIC PUBLICATIONS

CHAPTERS IN BOOKS

Montbriand, M. J. (2007). Positive findings about herbs and natural products action on cancer. In Ping-Chung Leung & Harry Fong (Eds.) ***Annals of Traditional Chinese Medicine***, *Vol 3 (pp. 179-232, Chapter 9)*. New Jersey: World Scientific.

Montbriand, M. J. (1997). Empowerment of seniors through improved communication about medication. In L. F. Heumann (Ed.), ***Proceedings of the Sixth Sciences in Health-Social Services for the Elderly and the Disabled*** (pp. 258 - 264). Chicago, Illinois: University of Illinois at Urbana - Champaign.

ACADEMIC PUBLICATIONS IN REFEREED JOURNALS

Montbriand, M. J. (2005) Herbs or natural that may cause cancer and harm: Part four. ***Oncology Nursing Forum***, *Volume 32 (1)*. Retrieved January 15, 2005.

Montbriand, M. J. (2004) Herbs or natural products that protect against cancer growth: Part three. *Oncology Nursing Forum, Volume 31 (6)*. Retrieved November 15, 2004.

Montbriand, M. J. (2004) Herbs or natural products that increase cancer growth or reoccurrence: Part two. *Oncology Nursing Forum September, Volume 31 (5)*. Retrieved September 15, 2004.

Montbriand, M. J. (2004) Herbs or natural that may decrease cancer growth: Part one. *Oncology Nursing Forum July 2004, Volume 31(4)*. Retrieved June 24, 2004.

Montbriand, M. J. (2004) Seniors' Survival Trajectories and the Illness Connection. *Qualitative Health Research, 14,* 449-461

Montbriand, M. J. (2004) Seniors' Life Histories and Perceptions of Illness. **Western Journal of Nursing Research 26,** 242-260

Montbriand, M. J. (2000). Senior and health-professionals' mismatched perceptions and communication about prescription and non-prescription medication. *Canadian Journal on Aging* **19 (1)**, 35-56

Montbriand, M. J. (2000). Health professionals' attitudes about alternative therapies. The *Canadian Nurse* **96 (3)**, 22-26

Montbriand, M. J. (1999) An overview of past and present herbs used for cancer: medicine, magic or poison? *Oncology Nursing Forum* **26 (1)**, 49-60.

Montbriand, M. J. (1998) Abandoning biomedicine for alternate therapies: oncology patients' stories. *Cancer Nursing* **21(1)**, 36-45.

Montbriand, M. J. (1997). An inquiry into the experience of oncology patients who leave biomedicine to use alternate therapies. *Canadian Oncology Nursing Journal* **7**, 6-9.

Montbriand, M. J. (1995) A biomedical perspective of alternate therapies chosen by oncology patients. *Saskatchewan Medical Journal*, **6(2)**, 5-9.

Montbriand, M. J. (1995) Alternate Therapies as Control Behaviours used by Cancer Patients. *Journal of Advanced Nursing* **22**, 646-654.

Montbriand, M. J. (1995) A decision tree model describing alternate health care choices made by oncology patients. *Cancer Nursing* **18(2)**, 104-117.

Montbriand, M. J. (1994) An overview of alternate therapies chosen by cancer patients. *Oncology Nursing Forum*, **21**, 1547-1554

Montbriand, M. J. (1993) Freedom of choice: An issue concerning alternate therapies chosen by cancer patients. *Oncology Nursing Forum*, **20**, 1195-1201.

Montbriand, M. J., & Laing, G. P. (1991). Alternate health care as a control strategy. *Journal of Advanced Nursing*, **16**, 325-332.